Anthony Coleman

SODIUM SUNSET

Limited Special Edition. No. 25 of 25 Paperbacks

Anthony was educated at 'Durford House School' in St Albans, Hertfordshire. He started painting in the 60s and taught at the 'Young People's Art Centre' for a while. He then qualified as an engineering designer and spent time at several headline companies. A few years ago, he took to the quill and started writing modern verse. Since beginning, he has been published in a wide range of literary magazines.

With dedication to Brandy. Cheers!

Anthony Coleman

SODIUM SUNSET

AUSTIN MACAULEY PUBLISHERS™

LONDON • CAMBRIDGE • NEW YORK • SHARJAH

A CIP catalogue record for this title is available from the British Library.

ISBN 9781528920810 (Paperback)
ISBN 9781528963206 (ePub e-book)

www.austinmacauley.com

First Published (2019)
Austin Macauley Publishers Ltd
25 Canada Square
Canary Wharf
London
E14 5LQ

Acknowledgements

The cover was designed using resources from Freepik.com and kjpargeter.

Synopsis

This is a selection of my poetry that has been written over the years. Two of these poems have been published for two poetry houses; however, I own the copyrights for the rest of these poems which have been unpublished.

The selection of poems have appeal to a broad scope of people from all walks of life and are intended to be thought-provoking. Some are happy, some are sad and some are very dark.

This collection is an initial introduction to my work, where I have many poems in my back catalogue.

Anthony Coleman

Here's My Hand. Here's My Heart

She'd not belonged...
   since painted wagons
worked the drove
steadied by the stockman's hand
   since blue-eyed piebalds
ran the beaten way.

The hollow where the brindle lay.

The kindled stove.

Her voice, a lilting descant to
a childhood world.

   Here's my hand.
   Here's my heart.

   My Roma girl.

   NB. Title is archaic form of Roma blessing.

Parallel Universe

It is illusory at best. 'This'
A singularity in which intellect
cedes to the interminable count
of rosary beads in the hope of
gaining entry into an even more
illusory. 'That'.

Priorities

I'd expected more.

The measured tones spooling
on a looped tape do not, somehow
seem sufficient justification for
the current situation.

My neighbour, an elderly man
stands in the doorway of his porch.
I notice, inconsequentially, that
he's forgotten to put on his cardigan.
It's a chilly night
I worry about him.

Overhead, barely audible in a cavernous
sky – the rumble of B52s.

The grass is cool.
A heavy dew soaks into the canvas
of my plimsolls.
I must remember to pack them with
newspaper so they'll hold their shape.

I light a cigarette.

A solitary star engages
my attention.

Summer Storm

I would not have thought
that it could be so bright.
Borne on the renaissance of
a late summer's evening –
a pipistrelle held in place
by splintered sunlight.
The freshness of raindrops
tingling against parched skin –
strung, like pearls, from
the eaves of crooked roofs.

Phantasm

They will tell you that it is illusion.
That a single light source projected through
the focal length of mirror 'A' onto the
surface of mirror 'B' will combine to create an orb of no
apparent mass held at a fixed
point in space. That it is a known optical
phenomenon – ask if the 'hologram' means
anything to you. They will tell you that it
is not the result of hallucination, nor is it
a cause for concern. They cannot tell you.
However, why it remains in place after the
light has been extinguished.

Specimen

It has become ritual.
The countdown from 5 thro 1…
7.2 indicated.
Technology which I do not understand
and which I do not fully trust
confirms that my blood glucose levels
are within acceptable limits.
That the prognosis is good.
That the insulin which I have injected
into my body is sufficient for purpose.
That it is unlikely that I shall slip
into hypo.

The room is small. It is painted white.

The familiar squeeze of my upper arm
though comforting, does not betray
the presence of a companion but, rather
an uncompromising systolic/diastolic 120/80.
The hypertension medication, which I am
required to take orally, is effective
and does not need enhancement.

The room is small. It is painted white.

In my wallet, I carry the requisite number
of donor cards, though I understand that
in certain spheres of society, my organs
my bones, may be traded on the open market.
It is a concept which I had not considered.

That of me which is valueless will be interred.
The room is small. It is painted white.

Unfamiliar faces framed in a plate glass
surround.
There is a stir of interest... almost
of affection.
I have been accurately carbon-dated.

The room is small. It is painted white.

Café Society

I sip latte.

Dismiss existentialism
as effete. (in a voice
pitched at just the right
level.)

Experience the percussion
of loss with a few close
of.

Discover Akhmatova.
(for effect.)

Resist the temptation
to dwell upon politics
religion – you, the last time
we met.

Resolve to feed the world's
hungry – recycle 85%
of my household waste.

Regard life obliquely as though through
a prism; the future, as
always, a point of conjecture.

Fable

Death is a badly drawn metaphor –
a fable – it is a peeling back
of layers – the return of innocence –
an umbilical stretching into the
middle distance – nothing more.

The Ballet

They dance, like charms
upon a thread of gold.
To rise, and fall
beneath the baton's spell.
Unblemished in the arclights,
soft embrace.
To swoop, and lift, once more
their wings in brief recall
of untold ecstasy.

Life Is Like...

A teardrop
tracking the face
of a clown.

Hourglass

Sand unfurls
small spirals circle warily.
thoughts are edged with glass
your silences grow louder.

CPN

11.45 am.
She sits just so.
Brushes crumbs from a sheet
of A4 paper sub-headed
'For' and 'against' balanced
on her knee.
Searches for the lighter she's
left at home,
in the car,
with the previous client?
Accepts that offered…
Exhales.
The subject matter is light
her movements fluid.
Designed to figure the workings
of impaired minds – to find out
what makes us tick.
Describing human behaviour in
terms of negativity, of depression
of getting smashed.
And
all the while
not knowing
that it's she who shapes the day
beyond that of the ordinary
sipping tea… turning.

It's then that I see, as though
for the first time, her face.

The curve of her smile.

CPN: Community Psychiatric Nurse

I Don't Do Butterflies

Butterflies are too beautiful
for this world.

> Like jazz painted
> wishes
> clinging to the sky.

> Doing that Icarus thing.

Long Distance

It is all a matter of perspective
of course. The way that the words
cling to the wire like migratory
birds, some chattering discordantly
in prelude to flight, others subdued
reflective, as if reluctant to leave.
each one diminishing in line of sight
until silenced by the click of a
receiver being replaced.

Photosynthesis

It's the way that chlorophyll
reacts with light.

Aspects, of the 'red'
and of the 'blue'.

Each heartbeat tracking that before.

No cornucopia or tambourine.
No challis raised or crystal ball.

Just footprints set in drifting sands.

In the beginning was the word.
And the word was...

$$6CO_2 + 6H_2O + light\ energy = C_6H_{12}O_6 + 6O_2$$

Falling

Lie beneath starfields
in the grip
of Isaac's nails.

        Engage.
        Focus.
        Accentuate.

And counting… 10
9
8
7
6
5
4
3
2
1
LET GO

NB. Think APPLES.

Leaf

I could see that it had been there
for some time, its finely veined
net trawling words from the depths
of long-forgotten prose; slipped
between the pages, perhaps on a
warm summer's afternoon when the hum
of insects, the rustle of dry leaves
had been the defining moment in an
otherwise uneventful day...
undiscovered until I had carelessly
taken the book from the shelf and
had held it open in the palm of
my hand; a fleeting braille set
against pages blanched in unaccustomed
sunlight.

I dared not move

        Lest the moment pass.

Words

Some are so fragile, I hardly
feel their loss, falling from
idle thoughts to gather dust –
twisting into small spirals
as doors open and close – rustling
underfoot in quiet moments.
Cast from the heights of unsound
Stanzas, they flutter their wings
through broken nights, scratching
at the edge of sleep till first
light.
Later, they'll be de-literated
by Dyson – survivors drifting
into forgotten corners, driven
there by the kids, the dog…
Some chewed beyond recognition.

Event

Just Chloe and me
and the three-inch refractor
A discernible red disc
held in the cross-hairs
of the sight.
Each lulled by the hum
of the equatorial drive, the repetitive
click of the SLR.
All but ignoring the soundless swoop
of an owl.
Stunned by the weight of starlight.
Chloe remarking how illogical
it was that such a creature
could move so silently…

kill so swiftly.

Hypothesis

Whether the concept of my being 'here'
is valid may be a matter of conjecture
though I remain in denial of not being
'there'; an attractive proposition not
to be resolved in the time allotted
where time itself is not constant and
where those of reason have failed to
determine a relevant hypothesis for being
other than a roll of the cosmic dice.

Published First Time in 52 Spring, 2007
Josephine Austin

Messier

Charles Messier, 1730–1817.
Catalogued galaxies and star clusters.

It seems to me that there are fewer
than there were. Perhaps, I should
have noticed sooner, but my thoughts
have been elsewhere. I have counted
them. I have made an inventory. But
there is always an imbalance and I
count them once more. The problem is
that I can never know exactly how
many have detached themselves, have
broken free. Every now and then, one
falls to earth and lays smouldering
in the outback or the steppes or a
housing estate in the north-east.
It is shown on primetime TV, slotted
between the latest celebrity expos
and sports desk.

        So insignificant a thing.
           I am concerned.

Girl

If only I'd seen you sooner.

A stickleback, beating upstream
against a white water tumble of
wire-heads, sees, reps, socially
inepts; the 4.48 – running late –
real-time.

Slipping through the shallows
and into my own reclusive
backwater.

A pre-emptive strike.

No three-minute warning.

No Clooney-jawed marine yelling
'Hit the dirt – Incoming'.

Just you…

Breaking surface tension with a
careless flick of your tail.
Coming to rest beside me in a whorl
of confusions, the platform
retreating into stunned silence.
And me, fumbling for words.
The remnant sunlight of a late
Summer's evening breaking over
flame-cut transepts.

You, assured, in control.

Chattering about your day.
The party you'd been looking forward
to for weeks. The shoes you'd wear.
Your ex.
How, perhaps. We'd meet again.
The tannoys crackling.

Your train coming in, slowing.

Your hand.

A long, cool, backwards glance.

A line of bubbles on the surface.

If there are no clowns in heaven
who then shall dance at our awakening?

Psychosis 1

Ah, so there you are…
filling dark spaces with
your avarice.

You come gently, as though
to be feared.

Friend… kiss me now
my breath is cold as ice.

Psychosis 2

Running…
through asphalt darkness.
Wrapping the silence around
her as she would silk –
heartbeats hollow against
the cold slab of fear.

Running

Always running.

Enlightenment

First were
the stones

then came
the words

and the stones held
the words in place

until enlightenment
When

the stones
were set aside –

held in place
by words.

Scuds...

Do not engage in discourse
of a moral or philosophical
nature.

Are not
passionate
dispassionate
rational
irrational.

Neither do they hate
reiterate
the creed of lost causes
nor reason with that
which is unreasonable.

Scuds describe sentinel arcs
of light through breaking skies.

Do not discriminate
do not reconsider.

NB. 'Scuds' are missiles.

The Men Who Dug the Universe

Kids played there
till the compensation culture
kicked in
and Health and Safety got involved
and the council put up boards
and the contractors wired it off
so anglers couldn't make it
to the swims and
relocated to the canal leaving
the banks to their own devices
till it was not cost-effective
for the council to maintain
till it was lost to memory
till it became as deep and as black
as the universe and
only the moon snagged in the branches
of a rowan, lit
the rise ring which reconfigured
clusters
A shoal of minnow sliding, unperturbed
Through starfields
The fall of a com-sat on re-entry
and the scally voices of those
who'd worked the pick long gone
No heroes, though, like Bevin boys
but ordinary men who'd scrapped a
living best they could –
piece-work then –
2/- a ton…

Published: Littoral, Dec, 2005
Mervyn Linford

High Fidelity

The strobe locks into the retina
dissolving into illusion.
There is no degeneration.
Wow and flutter have been contained
within acceptable limits.
Speakers exhale anorexic riffs into
fat silences.

Above the hiss...

Ella sings blues.

Sodium Sunset

Couldn't get a heavy today
all taken.

And the Chablis tastes like
Meths.

There's rain pouring from
a hole in the sky that God
could fix if He had a mind
to…

       but doesn't.

And backaways
a group of crackheads
have just achieved escape
velocity

       As the Krishna's
Mambo through snake pass.

       Instant karma.

       ****

In cyberspace
A pre-programmed binary
command travels at light
speed, along copper conduits.

****

The street lights come on.

Stasis

It is inconceivable that 'this'
where absolutes shaped by circumstance
impose arbitrary limits on the depth
of human psyche, could flourish in
the vacuum defined by reason.

Vanishing Point

Have you noticed how it is
with those old landscapes
where figures stand for
ever, looking towards a
point at which animals
and tree-lined rivers
conjoin, and colours
fade, receding into
blue, when animate
transforms into a
pixel dot? Where
nothing's as it
seems, shadows
interlace to
dance upon a
carapace of
light and
intercede
within a
satyrs
charms
alter
then
cut
to
0.

Whore

Daybreak's a whore
raising her skirts.

The one you took, drunk,
to bed…
        or another

    With smudged lippy
        Peeling lashes

    Who whined
        Yelled
        Scratched
        Beat you with guilt.

Until you, forgetting
            Sought the lining
            of another glass
            womb?

Point

Times you wake under
a blue suede sky.
Guys on point
breathin' like it's zero hour.
Pacin' the wire.
Finger on the trigger.
Go figure.
Feel not the nails.
Contrails
In a sky bereft of love.
There's nothin' left.
The orphan cries for love
that never comes.
Unsung.
An empty frame
a name
Unclaimed.

A Distant Star

The rise of tor.

A gown of grey.

Where clouds are snagged
upon the trees.

The valley's gaping jaws
engulf the night.

A distant star.

A candle's light.

Teardrops

Beneath the architraves
of light.

The glide of dove.

The baton held aloft
conducts the sanctity
of flight...
            As words transcribed
upon the heart in rhythm.

like wings, outstretched.

Do trace the teardrops
on a lover's face.

To...

To walk amongst the curvature
of dreams.

To trace the discord of the mind.

To dwell amidst the flight of time.

To raise one's soul into the light.

Hope

The turn of leaf
whilst falling.

Birdsong calling.

Star-dusted veils
of hope recalling.

A lover's fleeting
touch.

Skylarks

What games we'd play
'Neath sandstone skies
Where skylarks turning on the wing
Write quatrains clear upon the wind
With eyes bright, sharp of jet
Do gleam
In sunlight's joyous overture?

The Skaters

They stoop so low.
The hiss of blades on ice.
To glide like shadows
through the mist.
From Fenland dyke
to Cambridge Backs.
To barter eel.
At the market's keep.

Homecoming

Shall I but stay
Within this drift autumnal ley
Where dappled sunlight gathers
Fleeting soft
and fireflies sparkle, shimmer
briefly in everlasting twilight, dimer
now that night draws close
upon this place.
        Shall I but stay
In beechwood tangle, hushed, even errant
        Jay.
Entwined, the vines and tendrils beckon
to where the earth is soft.
Still that hurt within my breast
for here, I'll lay me down to rest.

Complex

You knew me once

And I, you

Now, in your eyes

I see only reflections.

Wireless

Voices flutter, oscillating against
a background of squeaks and whistles
the silk of '40s swing rolling like
breakers over attenuated frequencies –
dissolving into a foam of white noise
at first contact.

It's been like this for three days
An inversion layer covering much of
the UK.

Tentatively, I run my fingertips over
the face of the tuning dial – fixated
by the subtle glow of the magic eye
the opalescent green iris widening
appreciably at this unexpected foreplay.

Benny Goodman comes in through static
blows up a storm in the Azores.
The Dodgers have come out on top, again.
And from the far side of the moon
The plaintive *dit-dit-dit-da… dit-*
Dit-dit-da riding the short wave.

I turn down the volume. Dim the lights.
Settle back further into the armchair
listening to the rise and fall of oceans.

The magic eye opening… closing.

Maybe...

OK. So maybe, just maybe, today I'll
be different.

Maybe the dawn chorus of .410s being
discharged will be aborted.

Maybe bloodied bodies will NOT fall
from the sky.

Maybe we can fit the birds with wing-
mounted cannon so they can shoot
the fuck back.

Just maybe.

Embers

Quieter somehow
That part of me which once
was youth.
From gallop, now to gentler
gait.
No more the wake.
The tumbrel roll of wagon
stilled.
The smell of sweat, of saddle soap
the embers of our fire.

Tanka 1

Bright water

Enticing dabchick with

Fresh crust

In the shallows

A flash of silver.

Seasons

She'd gone in October.
In the churchyard, now
with the boy.
He'd not spoken of it
since then, the softness
of the earth prevailing
against the bitter word
the strike of spade on
flint enough to justify
a lifetime.
His hands held firm to
browning tops and braced.
A mounting pile of spuds
set fair to last the
coming snows.

Storm Force

They're here again tonight.

Their shrieks confound me.

Their fists beat against my dreams.

Their impatience grows.

Tanka 2

Dawn

A plough unfolding the seasons

Soon I shall wake and

Unaware

Dress myself in the new day.

Ghost

I saw you again last night
same time, same place
Coming out of the newsagents
head buried in the sports pages
not a care in the world
Totally absorbed in the outcome
Of the 3.30 at Chepstow
rating your chances on the double
the treble even
Swanning through life as you
always did
Heard the screech of tyres
the sound of the impact
(Third time this week)
Surely
you must've known
You were never going to get
the treble.

Haibun – On Childhood

Beyond the rise, the swerve of marram grass
the track winding down to the breakwater
the sea giving up its moods. A line of
footprints meandering over wet sands pausing
only occasionally to examine flotsam driven
ashore by the stiffening breeze.

> At the water-line
> A tingle of
> Expectation.

Anchoring the corners of the gingham tablecloth
with smooth white stones selected from the
many seeding the dunes. Sand whipping into small
spirals. In the lee of limestone outcrops.
All the while, a succession of cotton-candy
clouds building into thunderheads – an uprush of
gulls from the Martello tower flickering against
darkening skies.

> Summer storm
> A rainbow encircles
> My world.

And later, in the evening, walking along the
Prom. The sun sliding into the tropics.
Shadows lengthening into Viking longboats
cutting through the shallows. Making the long
slow, descent into gullies shaped by Hook.
Mist closing in around us.

Evening
Rockpools filled
With starlight.

I.D.

Each day seems less
Than the one before

The window growing
Smaller

Birdsong fainter.

Outcomes

It is conducted, dispassionately
by young men in freshly laundered shirts
who sip coffee, discuss eventualities
in measured tones.
Workstations are functional, understated.
Read-outs continuously scrolling incoming
interdiction rates I silo launch codes
predict scenarios with uncertain outcomes.

They sip coffee, discuss eventualities
in measured tones.

A mouse click away from zero.

Nine Months

We're told that it's intrinsically
safe, although some have doubts
That the atmosphere is benign and
poses no threat to our species.
That we'll find it brighter than our
present environment, less humid, but
that our eyes will adjust, our skins
adapt to the drier conditions.
We're told that life-support systems
will be shut down and that we'll be
expected to source, and maintain, a
renewable supply of nutrients.
(Our bodies will compensate for the
intake of solids.)
Most of all, we're told that the effects
of gravity could prove disconcerting.
That it could be a while before we're
able to stand.
We're told that the presence of other
lifeforms is not anticipated.

Circle

The only reality is that of our
own creation – death, a fable –
And, in our time, you and I will
pause, spend awhile in each other's
company – move on.

Two Haikus

Ebb tide –

The scuttle of hermit-crabs

At the water-line.

After the rain –

The smell of honeysuckle

And wild strawberries.

Biology Class

He'd been there since forever
his spit-honed knife blading
light into dull minds.
Explaining for the nth time
that certain lower lifeforms
were able to maintain basic
functions even after the heart
had been surgically removed.
I could've told him how it was
that Megan O'Brien, in the fifth
grade, didn't need to use a knife.

Fen

They're still to be found
of course
Barge painted wagons drawn
by blue-eyed piebalds.
Though there are fewer now.

Ponies
Pastured in the old way
brought on by men with gold
on their skin.

But the droves have become
the province of dog walkers
ramblers.
And the young men
Charioteers
drive 4x4s – use satnav.

Mostly, it lies in the fireside
banter of old men and in
the mist-filled hollows.

A silence edged by the echoes
of distant hooves.